Old Town New World:

Main Street and More in the New Economy

Old Town New World:

Main Street and More in the New Economy

By Jason Broadwater

First Printing: 2012

ISBN #978-1-300-00292-5

Prose Productions
125 Caldwell Street
Rock Hill, SC 29730

JasonBroadwater.com
OldTownNewWorld.com
RevenFlo.com

Table of Contents

"How wonderful it is that nobody need wait a single moment before starting to improve the world." – Anne Frank

Success in the New Economy

In this age of connectivity, there are 25 super-regions around the world to which all of the creative, educated, talented people are clustering. Richard Florida, author of the seminal work *The Creative Class*, calls this phenomenon one of the greatest human migrations the world has ever seen.

Inside those mega-regions, there are cities and hotspots of all sizes, which draw the talent in like bugs to a lamp. One of these regions spans from Atlanta, GA, through Charlotte, NC, to Washington, DC. Around each of these large cities are smaller towns/cities that are experiencing rapid growth due to proximity to these larger cities and due to technologies that allow work to be done in different ways than ever before. Thus, while the educated and talented are migrating together, they are not all crowding into the largest cities. For example, many people are moving to Charlotte, but many are also establishing footprints in the surrounding towns and cities that circle Charlotte like spokes.

I'm from one of these cities – Rock Hill, SC. It is just over the South Carolina line south of Charlotte and is very much part of the greater Charlotte economy. As I look (and travel) across the nation, I see so many cities and towns in familiar situations to that of Rock Hill. Whether 2,000 people or 200,000 people, each community both has its own unique qualities and shares a common story with unifying themes.

Some commonalities I see among such cities and towns are these:

The local economic development organization is in the unique position to pull together leaders from most every sector of the community.

Most cities and/or counties have some type of Economic Development organization in place, often more than one. What I see increasingly are the following organizations:

- an organization that is focused on industry that is county-wide or even regional,
- an organization that is city-wide, and
- an organization that is specific to the historic downtown and its revitalization.

These organizations are each capable of bringing together the most influential and powerful people from both the public and private sectors. This is a good thing, if leveraged well. Collective vision and coupling of resources can be very powerful to affect change. Yet, if these groups are plagued with group-think, rubber-stamping, and disconnection from the new economy, then the result is not a productive one. The key is to have the powerful from the status quo and the innovators of the future change mixed together in overlapping groups, as well as to have a productive and forward-pushing process.

City and county governments have much opportunity to work together in increasingly collaborative, coordinated, and effective ways. Often there is competition in economic development, even within the same county – from city versus city or even city versus county. This is not a good thing. The organizations need to be aligned, and mostly that alignment simply comes from sharing the same vision.

One strategy that seems to work well is if the county works on landing large employment relocations for the business parks, and the cities each work on economic gardening and talent recruitment and retention. The county can build, market, and upfit-to-suit spec buildings. The cities can support small business growth and work to revitalize their historic downtowns. These may seem less like collaboration and more like staying out of each other's way, but we've come to an era where a large company not only looks for labor force and tax breaks, but also good restaurants, arts, events, music, and other lifestyle components.

The revitalization of historic downtowns is widely acknowledged as a critical component of community success, but these efforts struggle to reach a tipping point.

The resurgence of walkable urbanism is as big of a cultural shift as was the movement commonly known as White Flight. White Flight was of course when the wealthier white population of our nation left en masse the urban centers of our communities and moved out to the suburbs. This migration changed the entire structure and nature of our communities. The interstate changed it further. The mall, even further. All of this change was based on leaving our urban centers, abandoning Main Street to the low-income clusters.

Downtown became an economic burden and a point of shame, or at least a place to avoid for the more economically healthy people in our community. Such a community structure created a further segregation among races due to the existing economic divide between them. The downtowns were quasi ghettos and the suburbs were flourishing. But all that has changed.

Today, we are seeing a great migration towards village-esque urbanism. The Millennial generation, for the most part, isn't looking to be in a neighborhood of clear-cut properties lined with "McMansions." They are instead looking for integrated living and walkable urbanism. They seek access to education, work, play, entertainment, green space, dining, and living all by foot and bike, all integrated into the same place. Density is no longer a bad word. Creative use of old space is the direction of the day.

Acknowledging this reality, communities all over the nation are making a concerted effort to revitalize their downtowns. Yet, progress in many cases is slow. It's difficult to open stores when there is no foot traffic, and it's difficult to get foot traffic when there are no stores. Offices with high-density of employment don't want to locate in a downtown without the restaurants and lifestyle to justify the investment, and restaurants can't stay open if people are not downtown in the evenings. There are chickens and eggs all over Main Street, it seems.

It is the village we seek - a cultural fabric and unique community at the center of our lives. But how do we grow our workforce numbers and strength in those spaces? Once you have the community will and the budget, it's easy to fix streetscapes and refurbish buildings, but how do you create or inspire jobs and wealth in a Main Street district? The answer lies in talent recruitment.

Technology and services sectors are growing rapidly in a clean, safe, manageable, and profitable way.

Professional services, educational services, medical services, commercial services, technology services... these sectors have grown consistently through the recession. Everything from back office to loan collection to telecom to Internet marketing to insurance sales and brokerage to financial advising to doctors offices to imaging centers and beyond. These businesses crowd the chambers of every community. These sectors are growing, and they are safe, quiet, and occupy space that can be green-friendly and integrated into a quality-of-life conscious environment. Each community is recognizing, embracing, and supporting this growth in its own way.

The local chamber of commerce has ample opportunity to serve and leverage the voice of the small business community, but struggles to stay relevant with new economy businesses.

Though much of a successful Chamber of Commerce's income and influence comes from its larger corporate members, much of its impact can be in fostering and facilitating the growth of local small business. Chambers often struggle with providing meaningful return for the small business member.

Often, the smallest businesses are plagued by their owners being hyper-focused on generating leads. I've heard many small business owners complain after a legislative luncheon that they did not get any time to network. Or attempt to justify the cost of chamber membership by saying, "Well, I didn't get a single lead from the chamber." The answer to this for a chamber is not to try and start leads programs or do more speed networking, but instead to embrace its role and clearly communicate to members that it is NOT a lead-generation organization. A chamber serves to empower small businesses by giving them a voice in larger conversations – conversations like those about legislation, economic development, and community direction. A small-business person can better understand these conversations, stay abreast of them, and add value to them through the chamber. A chamber has ample opportunity to participate in economic gardening practices that help foster growth among existing businesses by coordinating resources and facilitating connectivity, not by hosting a speed dating session for people to shove their business cards at each other. For example, allow a local document shredding company to give an educational presentation on the safety concerns of not shredding sensitive materials. Allow a business attorney to give an educational session on "Covering Your Legal Bases as a Small Business" or something of that nature. Education, facilitation of connectivity, and access and voice in the larger oceans affecting local business – these are the roles best suited for a chamber of commerce as it looks to serve its small business population.

A chamber is also a prime candidate to open and manage a cowork space. It's great for the revitalization of downtown, great for talent recruitment, and great for the chamber as it's one of the few ways the traditional business leaders of the chamber can be tapped into the creative services economy.

Higher education institutions are eager to demonstrate their direct relevance to economic development.

Due to high unemployment and slow economies, the educational institutions across the country are speaking more about their economic impact than their academic prowess. There has been a resurgence of conservative fiscalism at the municipal as well as the county council level, which often controls significant funds for technical colleges. Though this conservatism is in some ways responsible and needed, in other ways it can lead to limited, shortsighted vision. For example, economic impact is a bigger idea than the dollar amount it is usually distilled down to. The improving of the quality of our lives and the value of academic education goes well beyond our ability to earn a living or our community's spending around the campus.

While we need never forget that liberal arts education is the cradle of our culture, we are faced with a serious question about the value of higher education (as it exists today) in the new economy. Training programs, certificates, and code camps are popping up everywhere because traditional education can't keep up with rapidly changing technologies. And if the objective is to just get started doing a new type of work, then traditional education programs cost too much and take too long.

Higher education is facing radical change across the nation and globe, as well as working to find its role in each community. Three things come to mind immediately as ways higher ed can help and stay powerfully relevant - they can

1. serve to recruit and retain talent in a community,
2. integrate their development and growth with the downtown, and
3. gear their curriculum towards working on the needs of the community.

K-12 education not seen as the central important piece that it is, and it is being distilled to quantifiable measurements that do a disservice to the efforts to improve education in a meaningful way.

K-12 Education (and early intervention) is one of the most critical components of economic development of any community. As clichéd as it sounds, we must invest in our children's success as they are our future. Unfortunately, we don't seem to really believe that. We pay lip service to the idea, but we don't make decisions in a way that demonstrates our belief in it.

We should have the kids involved in all kinds of projects that support our community's growth. Let's teach them about their own town. Let's involve them in its becoming. We could use their energy, creativity, and work. Plus, it is very important that they graduate with a positive feeling and opinion about their hometown. This "my town is lame" phenomenon is a huge factor in putting suburban communities at risk in the new creative economy.

Also unfortunate, we have a movement in this country to try and quantify the results of K-12 Education down to a bottom line number. Thus, the efforts of K-12 Education become increasingly about affecting that number. When, truth be known, those numbers are only slightly useful. The success of education lies in the success of the children and the community they comprise. Confidence, innovation, experimentation, imagination, and persistence are the keys to the new economy, not regurgitated information. Knowledge was power. Now power lies in connectivity. The ability to use connectivity in creative and affecting ways is the new desired skill. Small cities that embrace creativity in education will produce more successful citizens for tomorrow. Communities that invest in children from the youngest of ages, will produce the most stable and productive environments. There is ample opportunity to bring K-12 Education to the front of the mind for economic development. We just don't seem to believe it is necessary. I suppose that's because we're thinking about the next 5 years, as oppose to the next 35 years and beyond.

*****

Often our definitions of economic development are too narrow. I believe that Economic Development is the effort to improve the quality of the lives of the citizens of a community. Each of the afore-mentioned sectors in a community has its own organizations and institutions charged with affecting positive change. Each sector is critical to the community's success as a whole. Thus, operating in silos is no longer an option. We must seek ways to collaborate at every turn. We must align our agendas and cnergy and work to achieve a true synergy – a better outcome for all of us. Collaboration is the overall character of success in the new economy. We need to apply different efforts to create a different reality.

Native Son Returns

Rock Hill sucks. That's what I thought as a teenager. *Rock Hill is awesome.* That's what I think now. How much did Rock Hill, SC, change? How much did I change? It's like that old expression: my parents got a lot smarter from when I was 17 to when I was 25.

Today, I often work with college students from the local university and technical college – Winthrop University and York Technical College – and I am very pleased to say that they don't think Rock Hill sucks. The Winthrop students especially seem to think Rock Hill is cool. And that's great news for Rock Hill, with much bigger implications for economic and community development than may be evident at first glance.

Rock Hill has a population of about 70,000 people and is located in the Greater Charlotte, NC, marketplace just over the border into South Carolina. The town has an exceptionally high quality of life... for most of us at least. We have a revitalizing historic downtown – Old Town, we call it – which is slated to host over $150 million of investment by 2020, mostly in the context of the birth of Knowledge Park. We have currently the largest mixed-use development in the Carolinas going in by the

Catawba River with an Olympic-approved Velodrome, an X-Games-approved BMX track, and new urbanism among them. We have a strong sports tourism sector. We have great schools. Thanks to Charlotte, we have access to "big city life" with its restaurants, culture, shopping, and more. Rock Hill is a wonderful place to raise a family and has been nationally recognized as such on many occasions. It's three hours from the mountains and three hours from the beach. It's a little piece of paradise right in the center of the Carolinas.

Yet, among this happy little image, our workforce numbers have not recovered since the recession. That's not a sustainable situation. Workforce numbers must increase as population increases, even without population increase. So, what do we do about it? Well… city staff can work to recruit businesses to this town with tax incentives and salesmanship. But that ain't easy. The game has changed, and we're trying to understand how it's different and what it means to us. The old ways of economic development aren't really working in the same ways in the new economy. One thing is becoming undeniably clear, we must have a local, organic, bubbling-up of entrepreneurs serving the new services economy. If we do not, we will not be able to continue our quality of life here in this place. The center will not hold.

I was born and raised in Rock Hill. The place I knew was a sprawling community of strip malls off I-77 with a serious inferiority complex to Charlotte. There was no historic downtown at the time, as it had been covered with a roof and turned into an indoor mall. No, really. I'm not making that up. To compete against the flow of traffic away from downtown and towards the malls, the City of Rock Hill put a roof on Main Street, laid down tile on the street and sidewalk, and turned downtown into an indoor mall. Then, the most regrettable piece, they tore down buildings to make much of downtown a parking lot to support the mall. Though city leaders' hearts were in the right place, the plan was ill advised from the beginning. If we wanted a mall, we could have built one. Demolishing and transforming our historic downtown into one was not a good idea.

Our city was also seriously racially divided at the time, and to a large extent still is. The mall was in a part of town where affluent people were not likely to visit, which is most directly a class issue but was inherently interwoven with racial divides.

The roof of downtown did not come off until 1995. To see downtown Rock Hill now is difficult to believe, as the downtown is beautiful and vibrant.

Back in my youth, there was not much of anything in Rock Hill, at least from the point of view of a teenager. I did not know the history of the place, at all. Only recently, have I heard about the historic hey-day of the Rock Hill Buggy Company and Anderson Motors. Only in recent years did I learn of the benevolent leviathan to bring jobs – Rock Hill Printing and Finishing Company or "the bleachery", which employed 20% of the population at one time. These histories were absent from my perspective. Only upon returning to this place did I discover them. Only while seeking to improve the place did I see their interwoven nature in our present here. And only when learning of my own family did I understand that this mill town with no mills is where I came from.

Born to mill communities, my parents very deliberately "moved up" out of Mill Rock Hill. This moving up, this upwardly mobile class ascension was, for them, the American Dream. The continuation of this class-climbing for me, as the next generation, was to leave Rock Hill – to get out. It seemed like there was this idea that leaving Rock Hill after high school was better and more associated with achievement, and staying in Rock Hill was worse somehow and more associated with lack of achievement.

This feeling of the hometown blues is partially part of the teenage phenomenon, of course, but the psychology of inferiority of place was reinforced for me around family, friends, and acquaintances – even out in the general public. And when I started going to high school in Charlotte, it was as if they were aware of it too. *Rock Hill Sucks* was commonly understood by youth in the greater Charlotte area and a less vulgar version of the same idea was reinforced by our parents.

When I went to college, the idea of Rock Hill being lame was far off. Rock Hill had as much potential in its vagueness as did any town. But to go back to Rock Hill, after college, would be to face the same notions of failure or lack of direction. That is not a judgment on the place as much as it is on me. That's what Rock Hill had taught me.

My generation's perspective on Rock Hill's inferiority complex wasn't the same as that of our parents' generation. Rock Hill wasn't inferior due to some blue collar / white collar tension. No, it was inferior mostly due to a lack of bohemianism – a lack of music, young people, girls, boys, restaurants, bars, etc. There was nothing to do here, and the town seemed to be lacking the progressive youth generation all together. Cherry Road was the main drag, and it was a small town mall, a couple of chain restaurants, and miles of strip malls. Most of the bars were the bars of the split generation (those who go to bars and those who don't) instead of being like the bars of the newer more mixed generation, where a bar is a tavern -- a gathering place, a restaurant, a music venue, and an overall positive social experience.

Essentially, there weren't any good, college type things to do in Rock Hill. There were some bright spots here and there, but for the most part, college students left on the weekends, and when they graduated, they took off never to return. Therefore, few independent restaurants and live music venues and events were able to ever get started because there wasn't the population here to support it. It was a self-perpetuating, chicken-egg-esque cycle.

So, I left Rock Hill, planning to never return, except to visit my parents. And I took my industrious nature and desire to create my own thing and do it myself, and I moved to Asheville, NC. I moved there for college, yet I chose the college because of the town. After I graduated, I stayed. I did not stay for a job. I stayed because Asheville is a compelling, dynamic, bohemian, energetic environment. I didn't know what I was going to do for employment. But I knew that I didn't want to live in Rock Hill, and that I did want to live in Asheville. So, I waited tables, worked in sales, and started teaching. Then, I started freelance writing through the Internet. And I started to build my own thing. I was driven to do it – to control my work, my time, my life. I wasn't looking to get picked up by some corporate entity who would give me a job. I was interested in creating my reality from scratch.

Then, my wife and I had a child. So, after much deliberation, we moved back to York County, and I found myself the native son returned. I didn't really know what to do with that. I knew that I was going to start my own business, do my own thing. I only ended up in Old Town Rock Hill because I found a building for sale for cheap, and I thought the downtown was compelling from an architectural standpoint. Also, I saw lots of potential in the downtown growing into something vibrant, something authentic and unique.

It wasn't long before I was stopped on the street by the mayor. He introduced himself and told me not to hesitate to share ideas with him and city leaders. I was shocked by the encounter and moved by the obvious sincerity in his words. A few months later, I was invited to participate on a panel of young entrepreneurs at an economic development meeting. I was consistently invited to participate from then on. This open channel of communication, the ability to have voice, this was very important for me. It was empowering, and it made me not only stay in Rock Hill, but dig-in and work to make the place better.

Bringing people like me to downtown is economic development one person at a time. We must do this to bring the creative services economy to our downtowns. We focus on the champions of change. I brought my own job to downtown (as we are in a bring-your-own-job economy). Then, I created 10 other jobs. I'm not the only one of course. Our downtown is now full of jobs, because we have successfully recruited the connectors who create them.

Work Not Jobs

For the last four years that I lived in Asheville, NC, I taught ninth grade English. I had had no plans to be a teacher, and I wasn't satisfied with that being my career. I wanted to own my own business or at least work for myself. So, I started looking for writing or editing work. I had an MFA in Writing and was teaching grammar as a profession, so I was pretty well equipped for a writing or editing job. I bought a book from the bookstore that was a catalogue of the writing marketplace, and I began to send samples and resumes to publications across the nation. Lots of postage. Lots of waiting. Eventually, I became impatient with the process and began looking for alternatives on the Internet. This was in 2002, so the Internet was a different place than it is today. It was less fluid and organized (it seemed). It was less ubiquitous in people's lives too. But, I found a website where I could bid on writing and editing work. So, I signed up. I paid the fees with my credit card. I beefed up my profile and resume. And I began to bid on projects.

The first project I was awarded was to copy edit and format a book for publication. I was bidding against vendors from all over the world, and I had no idea where this particular client was located. So, I contacted the client by email and asked how he would like to get started. He asked if we could speak on the phone. I said, yes of course. He asked what time zone I was in. I said, EST. He said, me too. He asked what state was I in. I said, North Carolina. He said, me too. He asked what city I was in. I said, Asheville. He said, me too. He asked what neighborhood or part I was in. I said, Kenilworth. He said, me too.

Well… it turns out he was in his home just around the corner from my home. We both walked out into the street and met each other in person there and shook hands. What we both learned that day, it seems, is that the Internet has no boundaries large or small. Each of us could have been anywhere in the world, yet we were only a few houses from one another. Even though we were neighbors, we still did all of our work by email. I saw him occasionally pulling into his drive and would wave. He was a nice guy.

In the macro history of the human experience, the Internet is an absolute game-changer. Like the wheel or fire or the combustible engine or the microchip, the Internet is more than a big deal. It affects the way we access information and communicate with one another, thus changing the human experience. It is changing how we migrate, how we live, how we play, how we work, how we learn, and how we create productivity.

We are in a new age – the Connectivity Age – in which our economy hinges on the creative use of communications, connectivity, and access.

So, after the one writing project, I did another. Then, another and another. Eventually, I was getting more projects than I could do, so instead of turning them away, I approached my competitors in those online bidding spaces, and I formed teams of writers. I then expanded the team with editors and a project manager, then an account manager. Then, when we moved back to York County, I quit my teaching job and went at this freelance writing thing full time.

What all of us in those bidding spaces had in common was this: we sought work, not jobs. None of us wanted jobs. We wanted work. With work, we controlled it. I could decide what projects I wanted to work on and at what rate of pay. Though, I had to win them, and that is not easy. But, the trade off was worth it to me.

Over the course of a few years, the web writing focus evolved into full web marketing services focus with the founding of my current company, RevenFlo. We developed a model with RevenFlo in which we provide web teams to organizations of all sizes all across the nation. The core of our business is strategy and project management. The next layer is talent with niche skills: designers, developers, writers, videographers, SEO managers, and more.

When we bring in revenue, we are essentially bringing in contracted work. It's like construction. When someone is hired to build a house, that is work for the builder, the project managers, the carpenters, the electricians, the plumbers, the masons, and so on. Yet, the construction/housing market is bust, and the technology and creative marketplaces are growing. Plus, this analogy falls short because the Web has turned into a fluid communications marketplace, thus needs of service are constant for most organizations. You don't build a website and move on, instead you have to put in place a team that functions on an on-going basis as your contracted staff.

RevenFlo is not alone in what we are discovering about knowledge teams and contracting. The model of the contracted worker and the flatter marketplace is all over the map. We are seeing it everywhere. Think of financial professionals who have been laid-off or quit their jobs to open up their own shops. Think of the health care professionals who are essentially independent contractors. No longer does an organization hire a janitor for 30 years, but instead contracts a team of cleaning professionals.

Also, the new worker is a knowledge worker. The new jobs are facilitation, management, and organization. The new assembly line is information and processes and communications. Thus, the new entrepreneur is the person who innovates in these areas, in these services models.

I recently went to Monster.com and searched 29730 (our zip code here at my office in Rock Hill), and here are the job titles I got as results to my query:

- Business Analyst
- PHP Developer
- Cost Accountant
- Web Application Engineer
- Lead Web Application Developer
- Sr. Java Developer
- Tax Manager
- Service Operations Process Architect
- Information Systems Architect

And you should see the job descriptions to these positions. It's all about knowledge, technology manipulation, and systems development.

The technology sector in particular is growing because it constitutes the support sector for the growth and change of every other industry. For health care to grow, for professional services to grow, they are looking at how to use technology effectively, to manage processes more effectively, to innovate and to create.

The new economy is a services economy, a technology economy, an innovation economy, a knowledge economy, and a creative economy. We see huge job growth in Educational Services, Health Services, and Professional/Business Services.

Here in York County, SC, we currently have over 11,000 independent contractors functioning as service businesses (according to Bruce Yandle, economist at Clemson University). These are 1099 contractors who are each their own business and function in the new services economy.

As the Information Technology sector grows (with huge increases in spending going into this sector from every other sector), we are seeing consultants and developers and coders and project managers and designers and writers and illustrators and administrators and marketing professionals (SEOs, PPCs, Copywriters, Etc.).

These are the service providers of the small business marketplace, with an estimated 70% of small businesses outsourcing web marketing, consulting, and development; and an estimated 55% of small businesses outsourcing their IT.

These folks are not all looking for jobs. Many of them are looking for work, not jobs. We hear politicians say, "Jobs, jobs, jobs." Maybe they should be saying, "Work, work, work." Work can lead to a W2 employee position or a 1099 contract or the hiring of a vendor. Regardless, it is employment for the worker and outcome for the consumer.

I believe that we, as knowledge workers, can ultimately work on the projects and in the capacities that are the most compelling and interesting and engaging to us, that we can best serve groups and ultimately our communities in the places where we are most passionate to serve. We can create our own lives and enjoy what we do, living a whole life, not one split between work and life.

My wife's grandfather is 89, and he always asks me, "How many people do you have working for you now?" He asks this because, to him, it is a measure of how successful I am to date. It shows how much power and responsibility I wield and is correlated to how much money I am making (which he would see as the key measurement on success, but he can't come out and ask me that, for it would be rude to do so). This man is not a shallow man or a callous man. On the contrary, he is a generous man who cares about enjoying life and family. Yet, he doesn't ask, "How much do you enjoy what you do now?" That would seem more of a measurement of success to me. And if in a longer more serious conversation, then he would agree. But he doesn't ask that because his question is about professional success. It's about work. My business. He's inquiring how my work is going. And he's trying to gage how much success I am having, and therefore, the most poignant question he can ask, from his point of view is, "How many people do you have working for you now?"

Of course, I know he is not looking for a dissertation on the shifting workplace of the new economy. So, I answer the question with "Well, we run 11 or so out of our Rock Hill office and more offsite." That answer satisfies what he's looking for, and we're able to communicate fine with that. But the real answer to the question is zero. No one works for me. They each work for themselves. We all agree to work together.

This is always true. No employee gets out of bed every morning for his boss. He does it for himself. He works a job because it is good for him to do so. It fits his life, his plan, somehow. So, really, everybody works for himself.

This shift in perspective is most prevalent in the creative services economy.

According to MartinProsperity.org:

- Approximately 1/3 of the U.S. labor force is employed in the Creative Economy.
- The Creative Class earns approximately 50% of overall income in the economy in the U.S.
- Creative Occupations represent 70% of disposable income.
- The Creative Class is expected to grow by 40% from 2006-2016. In the previous decade it grew by 30%.

Though the Creative Class is driving these Work Not Jobs shifts in behavior, contracting is also increasingly present in Financial, Legal, Health, and even the Commercial services. The real estate and construction marketplace was thriving off such models just before the bust.

The new economy need is knowledge-based / skilled labor. The new economy model is more focused on the individual, whether that individual is an employee, a consultant, part of a boutique service provider, or an independent contractor.

Many of these professionals can live in a small city and serve clients all over the area, region, nation, and world. These creative and motivated folks can gather and work wherever they choose.

Understanding such behavior and thinking is a critical aspect to success for a small city in the new economy. Success in the new economy is all about *The Connected Village*.

The Connected Village

I am often asked by communities, "What do we need to be successful in the new economy?" My answer is that it takes a village, and it takes the world. While this answer may seem cryptic, it couldn't be more literal.

For the past 60 years, we have developed this nation's cities simply as mechanisms for moving the automobile. We have replicated big-box and clear-cut projects to the point of cultural anonymity. We have compartmentalized our towns into working districts, living districts, shopping malls, and more. But a new dawn brings an embracing of our unique villages – villages of diversity and vibrancy, of economy and prosperity.

Rock Hill was born of the Industrial Era. As we grew, we supplied textiles to the nation, and by doing so employed more than 20% of our population directly, and much of the rest indirectly.

The backbone of this era was distribution infrastructure and logistics – interstates, airplanes, shipping lanes. Why make a million widgets in one town when the town doesn't need them?

You do it so that you can ship them all over the world and bring the money back home.

When you look at the flow of currency in the Industrial Age, you create an argument for manufacturing. You see the services economy simply shuffling around the same money in the same community, while manufacturing is bringing money from outside of the community. And this is what we need for growth. But all of that has changed.

The services economy now brings in money from the outside, as well. For example, the project scopes and proposals that are currently sitting on my desk at RevenFlo are for organizations located in Charlotte, Birmingham, Dallas, and Barcelona. They each describe services that we will provide to these organizations from our cozy little office on Caldwell Street in downtown Rock Hill. And the money they send us from their communities will be distributed among us, and spent at Millstone Pizza and Amelie's.

The backbone of the new economy is not Interstates, but the Internet. The Internet connects us to the world, from right here in this village. And let it not go unsaid that talent wants a village, talent needs the world, and talent is the core currency of innovation.

Rock Hill was founded in this spot because Ebenezerville did not want the train to come through their town. The White family and the Black family said bring it here, but give us a depot. That depot was our connection to the world. That connection created this place, for we built a village here where we had the world.

Today, the Internet is our railway. It's our connection. We have a village, and now the world.

The connected village provides the opportunity for people to bring their jobs to your downtown, to create their job in their own hometown, and to choose towns based on lifestyle choices. A cultural village is what we of the new economy seek, yet we can't afford to move to one unless it is connected to the global economy.

High-speed Internet offers the ability to create a depot in any historic downtown, to create a connected village.

The Punk Rock Economy

The coolest thing we had going in Rock Hill when I was a kid was Punk Rock. Our punk rock wasn't the punk rock of the 70s, of Johnny Rotten and the Sex Pistols, of anarchy and destruction. Our punk rock was based on openness and entrepreneurship. Our punk rock taught us that if you want to start a band, then just do it. You don't even have to be able to play your instruments that well... you'll figure it out as you go. If you want to be a writer and to read spoken word on stage, then just do it. If you want to start a record label or a fanzine, then just do it.

The dominant principles of the punk I knew were not destruction and nihilism, but productiveness and independence – to do it yourself... outside of the manufactured mainstream. You don't need to be sanctioned by some corporation. You can create your reality from scratch. Just start and see what happens. It was DIY Entrepreneurship, and we didn't even know it. We wrote our own songs, booked our own shows, rented out VFW buildings, and hosted kids from all over the Carolinas. We played shows all over the Carolinas and along the Eastern Seaboard and westward from there. We even recorded, produced, and distributed our own records. We created little businesses, made deals based on barters and handshakes, and sent records to each other through the mail. We had our own punk rock economy.

As young punk rockers, we were entrepreneurs, and many of the band members that I knew from the Carolinas Hardcore scene of the early 1990s are now owners and key staff in successful, entrepreneurial businesses, most of them located in the small cities where they were punkers (Rock Hill, Columbia, Durham, Raleigh, Chapel Hill, etc.). These individuals are driving their local economies. They want to control their own lives, and they are not motivated primarily by money. Money's important, of course, but not more important than controlling your time and finding meaning in what you do, and living and working somewhere that has life, culture, and bohemianism. These people have not changed; they're still DIY. But they are supporting their families now, and they are playing more significant roles in the organizations that affect our lives.

I've spoken to people from academia to corporate leadership to entrepreneurs, and I find commonality in observations made about the Millennial Generation. I hear things like... they want to control their time, they want to live and work in "cool" places, they are not loyal to a company as much as committed to a project, they seem less motivated by money and moving up, they need excitement and activity and change. They want to do-it-themselves. They want autonomy and to be encouraged to express themselves and explore their own ideas. These are the current challenges of the giant corporations, the small business, and the entrepreneur – to accommodate the needs of this workforce in order to capitalize on it.

You will find the Punk Rock or DIY spirit very present in new creative professionals and in the way they choose to do business. These professionals are attracted to and thrive in compelling, youthful environments. These are the entrepreneurs of tomorrow. We are told that the entrepreneur will save us. And I use that term sincerely in the sense that I believe our nation is on the cusp of being insolvent.

The new entrepreneur arises from culture-filled environments. They are not recruited to a town due to tax breaks. How much can a town offer a company with no employees and running 20 contractors?

What can a city do to bring in more of these businesses? Well, these businesses are DIY, grassroots, self-made, and punk rock at their hearts. We are finding our own way, creating our own model, and controlling our own lives.

We are industrious and productive and functioning outside of the corporate paradigm.

I am in Rock Hill because of its energy and potential. I see potential for an organic blossoming of bohemianism. We already have a vibrant underground music scene, a visible arts scene, knowledge workers, technology and creative companies, and some nice authentic restaurants. We have momentum. I am here because it's compelling and fun to be here. More entrepreneurs like me will arise from retained students. More will come when they find out about the compelling activity happening in Rock Hill. The growth will be organic and from the bottom up.

Tomorrow's economy is a services economy, a creative economy, an innovative economy, a contracting economy, a DIY economy, a punk rock economy.

Cowork as a Mechanism

To a large extent, the new economy is driven by two things: the creative class of workers and the influence of the Internet. While the Internet has allowed people to work remotely, it does not mean we all want to work alone. We don't want to work at home, either, at least not all the time. The ability to be mobile is important, and the creative inspiration and lifestyle improvement from being around other like-minded people is undeniable. One of the new creatures spawned from these factors is cowork. Cowork is a new way for people to work together in office space.

A cowork space is usually an open collaborative space that individuals or small groups share. The individual rents his or her work station, but as (or more) important, they rent access to the shared space and shared experience of working in a energetic environment. Shared boardrooms and presentation spaces, shared casual spaces with couches and comfortable chairs, shared kitchens and bathrooms, and large open spaces are the usual in cowork offices. Tenants can rent their station or office by the month or even by the day.

Cowork is growing fast. According to Deskmag, coworking globally has doubled in size every year since 2006. Of course, there are likely many more cowork spaces that stay below the radar of those generating such data.

The 2nd Global Coworking Survey, released in 2012, was conducted by Deskmag in corporation with Coworking Europe, Emergent Research, University of Texas at Austin, Coworking Deutschland, Coworking Project Italy, Jellyweek.org, Deskwanted, and Cohere Community. Over 1,500 people from 52 countries took part in the survey.

The survey revealed a wealth of information and benefits from coworking, such as positive productivity and powerful network building. As those of us who work in such spaces suspected, the study confirmed that the most important and powerful aspect of such model for working is community. 92% of those surveyed said they had increased their social circle significantly through coworking; 80% said their business network had ballooned; and 75% said that their productivity had increased, as well. When asked what they like most about coworking, 81% of respondents said the people.

80% of coworking spaces are operated as private, for-profit businesses with the remaining percentages dominated by non-profit organizations and only a small group (less than 5%) operated by governmental institutions.

We often think of such innovative models as for the bigger of cities, such as New York and San Francisco. But one of the fastest growing homes of cowork spaces is the smallest of cities – with populations less than 50,000.

For those who operate cowork spaces, the majority wants to expand and open more locations. Even with only 44% of those being profitable, they are still looking to expand, which speaks to cowork as often being a mechanism for something other than just its own sake.

82% of coworkers say they plan to say in the space for another year, and 65% say they have no plans to move at all.

Freelancers comprise the bulk of membership of cowork spaces. More than half of the freelancers surveyed reported a significant increase in income since joining their cowork space. 64% of freelancers in coworking spaces had worked previously at home. Others cowork members include employees and entrepreneurs (defined as owner/operators of businesses with employees).

Interaction is key to cowork. Many of the people working in these spaces get their work from one another. A designer can approach a developer and say, "Hey I have this project that needs PHP development. I hear that's your sweet spot, would you like to work with me on it?" Not only does work flow around the space, but knowledge and access as well. Professional development often looks like a few folks sitting on a couch talking about how something in the industry is changing.

This same cowork population also seems to be the people who frequent the coffee shops, attend the bohemian events, hang out in the pubs, and often play in the local bands. These folks are connected to the college scenes and energy, while making a professional living and having disposable income. It is this same population, as well, that seeks to live in apartments downtown. The idea of walking to work, walking to eat, and walking to play, is a celebrated idea among these populations.

Bohemianism and Urban Renewal

The impact of the creative class is bigger than just the jobs and the income. The creative class is the biggest driver of the successful revitalization of the historic districts of small towns across the United States.

Urban renewal in smaller cities is about the rebirth of Main Street. But Main Street looks different today. It's not stores that sell socks and underwear, but instead it's stores that sell crafts and pottery.

It's not mills that employ thousands, but cowork and keyman spaces that house tens. For example, in Rock Hill, SC, there is a refurbished Cotton Factory that now houses a student-loans collections agency and a marketing firm. The building houses more jobs today than it ever did as a cotton mill, and they are higher paying and cleaner jobs, as well.

Urban renewal is about walkability and lifestyle. It's about living and working in a neighborhood with pubs and coffee houses and dog walkers and such. There is a bohemianism about these places that make them compelling. This feeling, this culture, this spirit is why people want to work there, to build there businesses there. To be in the village.

I hear conversations among Economic Development leaders who are tired of hearing that a pizza shop is the answer to our unemployment problems, that a coffee shop with acoustic music will fix our economy. Of course, those little shops can't solve our problems. We need jobs, or work. We need feet on the ground, and then these lifestyle businesses can open and be supported by those who are here. Right? We need office workers and daily foot traffic to support the restaurants during lunch, which allows them to survive and thus be open in the evenings and on the weekends. That makes sense. But. What the new migration economy is teaching us is that we will lose our students and our youth, and we will not get newly relocated youth and talent if there is nothing for young people to do – no active, youthful, cultural center in the town.

We will not get jobs here because people will not want to come and work here, and businesses will not start-up here, will not move here, and so on.

We cannot underestimate the importance of lifestyle to this upcoming generation. Successful entrepreneurs will create smart businesses, and smart businesses will locate where youth and talent want to be. It's not driven from the top down; it's driven from the bottom up.

Look at the cities just here in the Carolinas that retain and attract youth and talent – Charleston, Chapel Hill, Asheville, Wilmington, and even Greenville (SC). These places have lots going on. They are fun, exciting places to be. These towns retain their college students and bring in recent grads from around the state and beyond. These people wait tables if they have to, but they want to be in these places, more than they want a specific kind of job. It's me in Asheville. I was there because the city is fun, interesting, artsy, and alive. These young, educated, people who often are the same people who have access to capital and support, are inventing the business models of the future. They are choosing to live in places that have the youthful energy represented by restaurants, bars, music, arts, etc. And they are creating their own jobs in those places. Young entrepreneurs want to be near other young entrepreneurs. They want to go out and interact. Cities with energy and bohemianism tend to recruit, retain, and develop creative talent. It's an organic, self-perpetuating, migratory process.

Talent, as well as businesses, will be attracted by openness and creativity. And yes, pizza shops and coffee shops and restaurants and live music create the environment that draws these folks in. But, it's a balance of symbiosis that is hard to strike. How long can a pizza shop stay open waiting for a critical mass? How do we reach a tipping point?

In Asheville, there is a part of downtown called North Lexington, and when I was there it was lined with shops opening and closing every 6 to 12 months. The rent was cheap, and a person could give their dream store a shot for thousands of dollars, not tens of thousands of dollars. If someone's attempt didn't work out, then they would have to close and move out of the way for someone else to try it. Over time, the ones that made it stayed, and now all of the buildings are full with strong, sustainable stores and restaurants.

We can't manufacture this type of growth. One way we support it, I believe, is with cheap space and loose collars. And by cheap space, I don't mean this fictional, bank-driven notion of "market rate" which seems to justify empty buildings. True market rate equals occupied. If that rate is not enough to pay the mortgage, then that just means the building is upside down. If we are looking to support business growth in Old Town, let's start by making the space cheap and see what punk-rockin', DIY entrepreneur dares to occupy it. We can't choose our businesses by type, instead we can make it easy for those who are interested to give it a shot. Even the energy of trying and failing is more compelling than emptiness.

Regardless of the shop owners, the presence of youth and bohemianism is an undeniable economic driver for a urban center because they create the environment that people want to visit and experience. Here in Rock Hill, Winthrop University conducted a study that they called the College Town Action Plan, which looked at the path towards Rock Hill being more of a college town. One of their discoveries was that in a vibrant college town the students only generate 20% of the spending in a downtown area; the other 80% is done by older, more professional or established individuals. Those individuals, though, come to the town to spend their money because they are attracted to the environment that is created by and for the students.

The Hive in Old Town

In the heart of revitalizing Old Town Rock Hill on the corner of Main Street and Caldwell, stands a 5-story, 100-year-old building that is tall and narrow and wonderful. The entire third floor, open with colorful columns in its center and windows all the way around, is a room warm with natural light and full of contemporary furniture and technology. This is the Hive.

Around 20 people gather in this space a few days a week, with handfuls of folks in and out on the other days. These people include students from York Technical College and Winthrop University, a staff from private businesses, and a couple of lab techs who manage the space. Also in and out of the space are clients, visitors, and attendees to student-organized events that take place in the space.

My company managed one of the training programs in the Hive since the space opened in 2011 until 2014. In this program, we trained Winthrop University and York Technical College Students (as well as a few high school students) to do website design by building free websites for non-profit organizations.

Beyond the synergy of the win for students and clients is the economic development component of the program. The city is invested in the revitalization of Old Town Rock Hill. Further integration with local colleges, student/talent retention, as well as new urbanism and place-making economic development are all primary objectives stated by city leaders and adopted by city council. Workforce development efforts that train people for a fast-growing industry is powerful work in economic development.

So, how did the Hive happen? Well, it took the investment of time, energy, creative capital, and financial capital from people, organizations, and institutions. But really, what it took most of all was for individuals who were friends to put themselves on the line. It took passion, friendship, and risk.

I was pushing this collaboration idea from the beginning to a large group of community leaders, but it was York Technical College that first invested the institutional component, which allowed the project to eventually launch at the scale it did. Then, Winthrop University came on board. Then, the City of Rock Hill. Then, a couple of sponsors – Comporium Communications and Harry Dalton. Once we had this powerful collaboration of people and institutions determined to see this thing through, there was no stopping us.

It's hard to really describe how much of a synergy the Hive creates. The outcomes are many, and they are intertwined in a way that generates unexpected wins of all kinds.

Community Development

The Hive clients are public sector and non-profit organizations that need web marketing outcomes to better perform their missions as organizations. They serve the needy or the abused or the neglected. These organizations are more effective in their missions due to working with the Hive. The Hive has created websites and Internet marketing programs for these organizations that allow them to get more stakeholder participation, more volunteers, more donations, and do more good.

Job Creation

The Hive creates jobs in several ways. The program not only trains the students of the program to be ready for working in an Internet Marketing capacity in the marketplace, but actually facilitates the introductions of students to potential employers. Many students of the Hive have moved directly from the program into gainful employment, either as a W2 employee, a 1099 contractor, or a self-employed vendor of services. Instead of students graduating and then turning to the marketplace to see if someone else has carved out an opportunity for them to vie for, we work the students as real workers on real projects for real clients, and through that they often create their own jobs that continue beyond the program.

Downtown Revitalization

Having the Hive in downtown Rock Hill is place-making economic development at its most powerful. Instead of creating a strategy on how we could potentially get students downtown, we just put their classroom down there and make them come. The energy injected into downtown by the students being there is impressive. Plus, the unexpected events and happenings driven by the students and their own desires to create and participate have been nothing but added bonus to the energies of revitalization in the downtown. They frequent the restaurants, the pubs, the coffee shop, and the stores. They are part of downtown now. I will say this is not because of the Hive; it's because of many such efforts, the Hive being one of them.

Institutional Collaboration

Another win for the Hive is to set a tone and create a model for institutions to collaborate for the good of the city and of the revitalization of Old Town Rock Hill. Bringing together York Technical College, Winthrop University, the City of Rock

Hill, RevenFlo, Comporium Communications, and the list of client-participants around this one compelling and innovative program has been inspirational to city leaders to work together and affect positive change. The collaboration is a visible win for each of the participating institutions, and such wins are immeasurably important.

Education is Economic Development

In speaking of success in the new economy, and of silos to synergy, I would be remiss not to speak of education, as it is a core piece of economic development. Economic development is the effort to improve the quality of life of the citizens of a community, and there may be no greater factor in this effort than education.

Higher education is currently struggling with its own funding and justifications in the face of our slow economy. How does academia support job creation? This seems to be the most common question I hear at the meetings I attend. Yet, we do ourselves and the quality of our lives a disservice if we think that academia should be only about workforce development. There is no measure of the value of History, Literature, Arts, Pedagogy, Philosophy, and more. These studies provide mechanisms to pass along our culture and our collective learning as a people. We need to make sure that our fiscal conservatism, though needed and welcome in many ways, does not make us naïve and superficial in this life of ours. We are here for meaning, joy, and beauty. Jobs are just a mechanism of sustainability. Life is about living.

Workforce training is an easier nut to crack for the technical college when it presents to its funding organizations because it is usually built right into the school's mission and purpose. Though, this is an ironic situation due to the statistics that state that the job growth for positions that require a masters degree are set to increase the most – much more than technical degree jobs.

As these institutions of higher ed jockey to position themselves as relevant in a slow economy, the K-12 schools do the daily work of educating ALL of our children. They have no choice in the matter. We as a nation have declared that we will educate everyone. It is each person's right to be educated, we have decided. And the schools are charged with making that happen, no matter what.

While still living in Asheville, I taught ninth-grade English in the small town of Marion, NC, for four years. I had never studied pedagogy before applying for the position. And actually, when I met with the district HR supervisor, I pronounced the word incorrectly (with a hard G at the end) and asked what it meant. She kindly replied, the study of teaching. Not only had I not studied in the field of pedagogy, I had never even taken an education class in my college career. But, I had a Masters of Fine Arts in Writing and a Bachelor of Arts in

English, so I met basic qualifications to be hired by the district. More than my resume, I fit the bill of a young, talented, creative, dedicated person who could potentially bring the positive change to the school that the principal at the time was seeking.

The interviewing team had no idea that the day before the interview, I had hair down to my back, a dreadlock in my head, and a burley goatee. They saw a clean-shaven, short-haired, well-dressed young person with a strong academic record, and they decided to take a chance on my ability to teach.

I embraced teaching and did well at it. I quickly learned that success was not about the content. It was about connecting with the kids. Kids can't learn if they can't connect with either the teacher or the material (hopefully both). The true learning happened in connectivity. Today's education is not a transferring of knowledge, but a preparing and practicing of using connectivity and information in meaningful application.

While I was teaching, *No Child Left Behind* passed through the legislature, and everything at our school became focused on the standardized multiple-choice test. The quality of the learning experience went down, as the test scores went up. The purpose of us being there evolved into the manipulation of those scores. I became unhappy with teaching and wanted out. The nature of education was being pushed back to knowledge transfer instead of meaningful application and exploratory thinking. We were going in the wrong direction.

We've all heard for a long time that the U.S. is behind in education. We've heard of the international standardized tests that our children do poorly on and Asian children score well on. But we forget that we saw the same thing as compared to the Soviet Union, and how did that work out for them? If we do so poorly in learning and preparing for our future, then why have we dominated the world's economy? Why do we have more innovation than any country by far? Why are Asian countries changing their education systems to look more like ours?

Well... maybe these tests measure the wrong thing. They measure the transfer of information. They don't measure confidence, ability to innovate and think for oneself, ability to fail and try, try again. These are the qualities of the entrepreneur. These are the qualities of the innovator. The person who drives productivity in this nation is not a know-it-all, is not a memorizer, is not even a rule-follower. The innovator in this nation is someone who challenges the status quo, someone who thinks for himself, someone who dreams about doing the impossible, and someone who is willing to fail over and over again, and never give up.

The economic development community needs to get involved in supporting K-12 Education and needs to take a vested interest in how we measure the success of our children and our schools. We do not need to be led in this regard by legislators who from their distant chairs try to apply quantitative measurement principles that push learning back towards knowledge transfer. It will be to the detriment of our communities in this new economy, this new age of connectivity.

A Strategy for Success

If you are involved in the work of economic development for your city or town, whatever the role or capacity, then this strategic framework is for you.

We can inundate ourselves with information, perspective, and ideas around the new economy and still not know what to do about it. Often, it's difficult to affect change without having a strategy that everyone involved (individuals and institutions) can "sign off" on. Then, the support for specific actions can be garnered because those actions can be shown as relevant to the specific approved strategy. Such strategic alignment can facilitate specific investment, projects, and actions, and is therefore a powerful agent for affecting positive change in a community.

As a strong example of this strategic alignment process, consider the Knowledge Park project in Rock Hill, SC. We are seeing radical change and the beginnings of hundreds of millions of dollars in the historic urban core of the city.

It was about 10 years earlier when we had our first conference of our contemporary conversation about revitalization and energy in Old Town and the economic development benefit of urban revitalization. We've done a lot of meeting, a lot of studies, and a list of very innovative projects since then. All along, we were building a vision through participation. As more people see the vision, it begins to emerge as our reality, to manifest through ideas becoming projects for change – either private sector, public sector, or through collaborations and partnerships.

As you approach your community in the context of the new economy, you will surely need to seek strategic alignment around these ideas delineated below. I hope these help you in your work for positive change and success in the new economy.

Feed the Center

The first philosophy to imbed into everything you do for the new economy is to feed the center. Imagine a balloon. You don't expand a balloon by pulling its edges out. Instead, you blow into its center. Then, the balloon expands. I heard this metaphor somewhere (maybe read it somewhere, not sure), and it has left a lasting impression on me. At RevenFlo, we operate our business on this philosophy. We call it the RevenSphere. At the center of the sphere is us, around us are our clients, then our prospects, network, and community.

We start every day looking from the center. What am I doing? How well am I doing it? What am I trying to achieve? Which brings us to clients: For whom am I trying to achieve it? Why is it valuable for them? Then, we go out a rung and look at our prospects. How can we help them be successful and therefore move them towards the center to be our clients? Then, we go out to our network, then our community. Always seeking to expand the sphere from its center.

Often businesses will invest heavily in sales people and presentations and focus on acquiring new clients. This focus is sometimes to the detriment of taking care of their current clients. This is bad business and leads to a dysfunctional type of growth that is less about people and more about quotas. Always start by putting energy into the center. That is the primary place to invest.

In terms of a community and its economic development, this philosophy should be the same. Put your primary efforts into the center of the sphere. Who is already there in your community, already making a difference? Are there people already opening restaurants? Are there people already holding events? Are there people already expanding their businesses? Are there people putting on music shows? Approach the people who are already doing something that looks like growth and activity. Those people are driven by an internal passion to do such work. Those are the people who should be first to be considered for partnership, help, subsidy, etc. They are proven catalysts who have chosen your community for a variety of reasons. Often, we take these folks for granted while we seek out new possible relationships and businesses and tenants and partnerships. The new partnerships will often come from the existing ones. The entrepreneurs in your downtown, the businesses in your business parks, the students at your colleges... invest your time and money in them first.

Revitalize Your Urban Districts

Most every small city has a historic downtown or some kind of urban district or historic center. The revitalization of this urban core is absolutely critical to the success of your city or town in the new economy.

Here in York County, Rock Hill is our economic center, but our small capital is called York. This sleepy little town recently formed an economic development group and met with the director of the countywide economic development board (YCEDB). The members of this newly founded group asked the YCEDB director what he thought they should focus on. He said, "Revitalize your downtown." The YCEDB competes globally for business relocations, but they know that these decision-makers want more than tax incentives and logistics. They want restaurants and quality of life. They don't want to move to a place without an interesting downtown to visit. Small is not a problem. Empty is.

Aside from supporting business-recruitment economic development, a vibrant downtown is place-making economic development, which supports talent recruitment, talent retention, tourism, and more. The whole city is affected most by its urban core, especially due to the inward migration we are seeing across the nation.

Once you decide urban revitalization is critical, then what? It's not easy, that's for sure. But think of it in pieces that work together. The pieces are:

- Office
- Restaurant
- Retail
- Residential
- Events

You must have people. People come before any private-sector restaurant or retail venture can survive. Office brings people who can make their living based on the nature of their respective businesses and not dependent on the vibrancy of the downtown (or foot traffic, so to speak). They bring their own job. Meanwhile, they create the beginnings of a vibrancy in downtown. Also, they can spend their lunches and after hours in the downtown, as soon as there are restaurants and pubs to support it.

Consider bringing a business park mentality to your urban core and recruit high-employment uses to your downtown. Market it like a business park to high-density, high-pay services – financial, medical, back office, professional, technology, etc.

Also, look at creating or facilitating some innovative office options and solutions – such as keyman offices and cowork spaces. These spaces retain professionals and bring them out of their homes. These spaces can also be fed by incubation programs from the local colleges and universities.

Restaurants should be left to the private sector. Probably the one exception is if your community college or university has a culinary program. If so, consider setting up a restaurant in your downtown run by that program. Otherwise, it's up to the private sector. If there are enough office workers, then an entrepreneur restaurateur will open a lunch spot there to capitalize on that population. Just make sure that your laws, regulations, historic preservation, and necessary regulatory agencies are all positive in their stance and approach. Government employees and processes need to be a helpful and eager part of achieving success for the private sector, not a series of complex roadblocks. Consider forming a department downtown that helps an interested business owner navigate any and all regulatory processes that he or she may face in the process of opening and operating a business in your downtown – a one stop shop. Don't allow government employees to send someone away because their problem is for a different department to handle. This has a debilitating effect on the small business.

As long as the process is simple, restaurants will open and succeed based on the lunch crowd. Then, they can stay open in the evenings and weekends helping that time of the day and week become more vibrant in the downtown.

Retail

Retail is a tough nut to crack. For a fledgling downtown, a retail store will find it is almost impossible to be profitable, and profitability equals sustainability. If a retail tenant can be secured that it is a destination retail store – something that has an audience who drives from a wide range of distance to come to that store already, wherever it is located – then the store can be successful and contribute to the downtown. Other stores can then piggyback off this success, and growth can occur.

There are also opportunities to create gallery spaces where local vendors would come in and rent booths. These could be arts and crafts or other things, as well. These spaces can be operated all the time, or just on weekends, or just during events. The model will depend on the town, but regardless, they can bring retail energy and people into the downtown.

Residential

Every downtown needs to have affordable, nice, compelling apartments downtown. By affordable, I mean something a 25 year old with a good starting technology job or contracting gig could afford. By compelling, I mean high ceilings, brick walls, natural light, and other such admirable qualities that bring a "cool factor" to the space.

One way to help make an apartment project go vertical is to have a local business step in as the anchor tenant for the ground floor. Such a commitment goes a long way to making the deal pencil. If the private sector cannot put forward such a champion, look to your colleges and universities. Can they put a classroom, incubator, program down there? Can the city justify the office space? Who can?

Events

We have to move away from this notion that events in a downtown is a lifestyle thing, and that developing buildings is an economic development thing. They are the same thing. High-tech companies and entrepreneurs will locate in a downtown because of the talent, and talent wants to be at the pizza place, in the cool apartments, and at the events that happen downtown (as long as there are cool bands and not just "old-people bands"). Also, the young family demographic will come downtown for family friendly events, and the active adult community will come downtown for events that appeal to them.

Events are a great way to get people downtown and show them what is going on. Be sure to take advantage of having those people there. Be sure to work with your restaurants and retail stores and make sure they are open and prepared. Be sure to have kiosks and information about projects that are coming to the downtown to generate buzz about growth and movement in the downtown. Good events are good investment for the revitalization of your historic downtown.

Arts and Architecture

Remember that the participants in the new creative services economy choose a place based on wanting to be in that place. They can either bring their own job, or hope one opens up for them among the others who came to that place. They seek the village. The physical nature of the place and the way in which its culture is embedded in that nature is the most important aspect of place. People create culture and place simultaneously. The cultural fabric of a city is interwoven into the architecture, public spaces, and public art. These are not after thoughts. These are prime drivers of growth in the new economy because they are key definers of the village, and the village is at the heart of our new world.

Invest in making great places. Everyone in your community benefits. Jobs follow.

Embrace the Internet

It's hard to overstate the importance of the Internet in the new economy. We are in the Connectivity Age, and the primary mechanism of connectivity is the Internet. There are two major sides of the Internet to consider in your economic development efforts. One is Internet access. The other is the use of the Internet as a marketing and communications tool.

Internet Access

Embrace the fact that most all of the businesses that will locate in and around your urban core need Internet access. Potentially, they need a lot of bandwidth as well. Your community must have an option for businesses to have high speed Internet access without much hassle or difficulty.

Also, if you really want to use the Internet for economic development, then have your historic urban core lit up like a Christmas tree with free high speed WIFI. If every home and business in your urban district had free access to powerful Internet, then you'd see a significant relocation to that area.

Plain and simple. Be creative in making that happen. It will be worth the investment. Water, Sewer, Electricity, Internet.

Internet Marketing

Every city needs to market their properties, speck buildings, business parks, and historic districts online. A city must market assets, benefits, successes, news, opportunities, and more. The effective use of the Internet to tell interested people about what is going on in your city is one of the most critical aspects of successful economic development in the new economy.

Story telling is key. Tell your story by telling your stories. Keep a constant flow of content outbound from your community about the successes of your citizens and their ventures. Success attracts success. Use the web to tell your stories and to listen to people's responses. Carry on meaningful conversations with interested individuals online about the successes in your community. This is what powerful community marketing looks like today.

Partner With Higher Ed

The city and the institutions of higher education should look for multiple ways to work together on economic development. The most obvious way for this to happen is for the educational institutions to locate classrooms or programs in the historic downtown. Other ideas have to do with programs where students do work, as part of their capstone experiences, for the public good of the community. For example, if your local technical college has a strong nursing program, then look to create a program in your downtown where nursing students offer services to people in need in the community for no charge. Not only do the students gain a powerful experience, not only do the needy get valuable services, not only does the downtown get a place-making boost, but the city can get much positive PR from the program and potentially recruit medical services businesses who want to locate near this program and its successes.

Higher education is a major employer and a major talent recruiter for any community. These should be capitalized on by the city in ways that benefit all involved.

Partner with K-12 Schools

I believe it is to our own shame that we as communities in this nation often neglect K-12 Education as being the most critical aspect of economic development. Those are the future citizens of our community. There is no more important work to be done than to make sure that we are preparing successful and happy people to live in this community. We should be teaching our children about our community, the history of the community, and about economic development principles. We should have students participating in programs that help the needy, as well as programs that explore our city's culture and arts. We should have people involved in making our city a better place from kindergarten on.

Here in Rock Hill, city council considers one single question at every decision point: Is it good for the children? This is a great step for the leaders to consider the children. But we need to take it further and have the children consider the city.

Recruit Servant Leaders

The leaders of economic development for any city should spend more time recruiting and facilitating servant leaders from the community than vetting and working with consultants. Your own community knows what's best for itself. You just need participation and process. You should form advisory boards and committees of local leaders. Make sure they are not just rubber stamp groups or time wasters. Really find ways to put these eager folks to work for the good of the city. It is more difficult to create meaningful avenues of productivity for volunteers than it is to just do work yourself. But you can achieve way more if you leverage your time to facilitate many minds and hands instead of just your own.

Encourage a Thousand Voices

When I was in Asheville, I was part of an arts scene that was connected to the University but flourished behind the Green Door. The Green Door was a wonderful venue in Asheville of which limited amounts of people were even aware. The entrance to the place was down a narrow alley and behind an unmarked green door. The venue held one-act plays and poetry readings and gallery events of all kinds. The scene was a DIY scene, independent to the core.

I loved the place and would attend events there and even hold events of my own there, in conjunction with the owners. There were many other scenes like that in Asheville, and it was the combination and synergy of them all that made Asheville the vibrant place that it was and still is today.

I remember when the Arts Council came to downtown Asheville and began to write sponsorships for such venues and events. At first, that was welcome, as each scene appreciated the support. But what began to happen was that the Arts Council began to control much of the events, just due to their part in providing funding. They began to coordinate and bring together various scenes under a strategic umbrella. Luckily for

Asheville's sake, the scenes were too strong and just continued to do their own things. If they would not have been so strong and vibrant in their individuality, we could have ended up with an arts culture in Asheville that was controlled by a committee... disaster.

Vibrancy is the clanging of a thousand voices, not one single voice. We have a tendency in our desire and efforts for strategic alignment to think that we must pull all the efforts into one. But to do so means to have fewer and fewer people in control of the destiny of a city, and that's a bad thing. Single individuals or groups do not have the creative capacity to control the direction of the growing vibrancy of a revitalizing downtown.

In Rock Hill, Old Town is one thing, but not controlled by one voice or one entity. We need a thousand voices, a thousand entities. That is Old Town. The place with a thousand voices. We need to help connect those who want to work together, help connect people to resources, and help put a megaphone to the noise that arises from the clatter. We do not need to try and organize all that is happening into a neat little plan, package, and voice. We do this under the call of Strategy. We've all taught each other for so long that strategy is key. And I am even putting that forward in this book. But I mean a different kind of strategy. We don't need a $65,000 3-ring binder with all the usual language and headings. We need instead a vision. Then, we can create tactical plans… that is our strategy.

We must think like an entrepreneur. Does that mean you jump in blind? No. Instead, you have a vision of where you are headed, and you focus on the tactical implementation activity that bears fruit immediately (or in the nearest spring). While doing this, you remain self-aware, market-aware, and you learn from what is working and what is not. Agility, diligence, innovation, and talent… these are key.

As this applies to your historic downtown and urban center, just start by plotting all the properties, projects, and potential. You know what you want: High-density, high-tech, mixed-use, walkable urbanism. Then gather together your champions and ask them what they need. That's the strategy right there. Let's put some project ideas on the table and get started.

About The Author

Jason Broadwater is founder and president of RevenFlo, an Internet Marketing and Web Development agency in Rock Hill, SC.

Jason is also founder and director of Old Town New World, an initiative to revitalize Main Street USA in the context of the new services economy (which includes among its projects the breakthrough tool AdayRemus.com).

Jason speaks and writes on "the connected village" and is the author of 5 books.

Jason is of the 2014 class of Harvard University's John F. Kennedy School of Government for Innovation in Economic Development. He has a Masters of Fine Art in Writing from Goddard College in Vermont.

Jason serves on the Economic Development Board for the City of Rock Hill, as well as other boards and committees in the region – the Steering Committee for the Technology Incubator in Knowledge Park, the Upper Palmetto YMCA Corporate Board, the Advisory Board for Piedmont Medical Center, and more.

Jason is married to his life-long best friend (Dicksy) with two children, Drake and Rosey.

Contact Jason at jason@revenflo.com or 803-328-6033. Visit JasonBroadwater.com, OldTownNewWorld.com, and RevenFlo.com.

Praise for the Author

"Jason is a compelling speaker and writer full of innovative ideas. His notions of collaboration through public/private partnership and bringing together Education and Economic Development and the Internet are cutting edge and worthy of note by those of influence in these sectors." – **John M. Papadopulos, President, Wells Fargo Retirement**

"Jason is a visionary person with a remarkable ability to put ideas into action. In supporting economic development of Old Town Rock Hill, Jason has created an annual conference, has built partnerships with York Technical College, Winthrop University and the City of Rock Hill to create The Hive, and served as a board member and committee chair for Rock Hill Economic Development Corporation. And along the way, he's built a growing, successful business. Highest recommendations!" – **Stephen Turner, Director Economic & Urban Development, City of Rock Hill SC**

"Our partnership with Jason is critical to us. I love talking with him about my ideas for not just communicating what we do, but how we can improve. He always challenges me to take it one step further!" – **Dr. Lynn Moody, Former Superintendent, Rock Hill Schools**

"Jason's leadership is bringing a new energy, youthful energy, to the core of Main Streets of Old Town." – **Harry Dalton, Philanthropist**

"The Horry County Schools has found Jason to be extremely forward-thinking and innovative. He has been extremely helpful in guiding leaders in this community to plan for new ways to connect and link our resources and talents to better serve the entire county." – **Dr. Cynthia C. Elsberry, Superintendent, Horry County Schools**

"The best seminar I was privileged to attend in the past two months. Jason was unreal good and the info he gave us has already had a positive impact on our town. It was a game

changer for Federalsburg. Good job. No, great job. Thank you."
– Bill Beall Mayor of Federalsburg, Maryland

"Jason's ability to convey the message of how crowdsourcing can be used as a tool to spur redevelopment efforts is uncanny. He has made the connection between public engagement and community redevelopment. I encourage you to hear him share his experiences in Rock Hill, SC." **– Wade Luther, II Economic Development Director, City of Camden SC**

"The program Jason brought to our community represents the very best of today's reality. A joint effort with the public private and educational interests combined to enhance economic development and learning experience is a win for everyone. Our hope is that the quality of life in our community and this new high tech initiative will result in creative jobs in a place young people will want to stay and call home." **- Doug Echols, Mayor of Rock Hill, SC**

"Jason Broadwater is received like a "Rock Star" in Easton, Maryland. His message describes how connectivity is changing the economic development dynamic in small rural towns. Jason provides a compelling outline for what we all know intuitively, but must act upon as a community, that we must create work – not jobs – so that people can come together and contribute. I wish I could bring Jason back on a regular basis to provide the energy and optimism that he brings to any room." – **Paige Bethke, Economic Development Director, Talbot County MD**